Your Mind is a Garden

By Lacey L. Bakker

For Denver, Harper, Harvey, and Myles,
You are the seeds of my greatest joy, the blossoms of my brightest days. May your minds always be vibrant gardens, filled with good thoughts, wild dreams, and endless possibilities. Remember to nurture the beauty within and let kindness bloom wherever you go.
With all my love,
Auntie Lacey

Published by Pandamonium Publishing House
www.pandamoniumpublishing.com
pandapublishing8@gmail.com
ISBN: 978-1-998467-14-3
Published and Printed in Canada
First Edition: January 2025
For permissions, inquiries, or additional information, please contact the publisher at the email provided above.

This part of your mind is awake and thinking on purpose. It decides what seeds to plant in the garden.

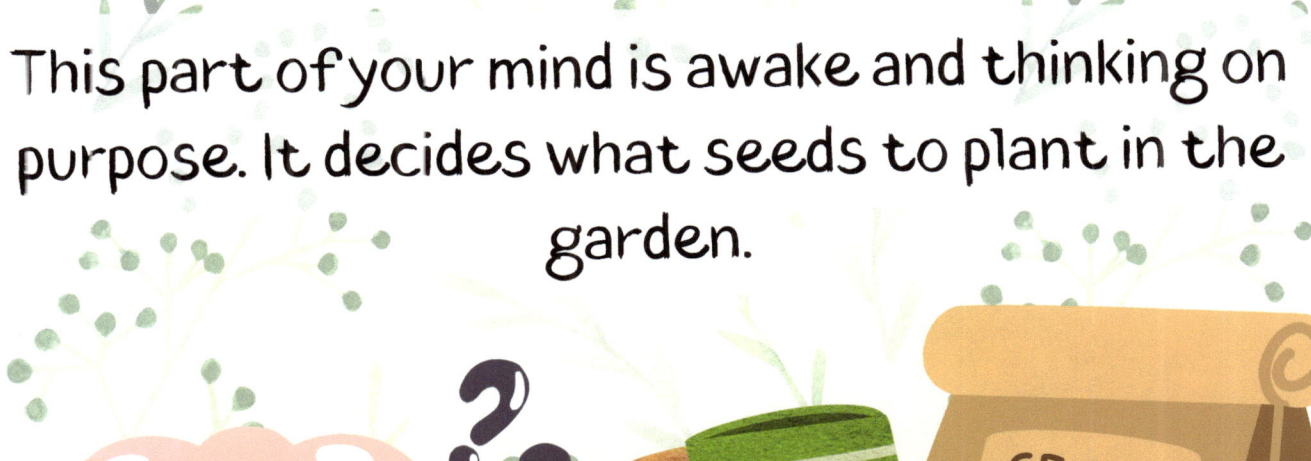

The seeds are your thoughts!
"I want to be brave!" or "I'm scared of spiders!"

This part of your mind stores all the seeds (thoughts and beliefs) that the gardener planted.

It doesn't ask if the seed is good or bad. It just makes it grow—because that's its job!

If the gardener plants "I'm not good at math," the soil grows that belief like a big weed.

But if the gardener plants "I am strong and smart," the soil grows a beautiful flower!

Your subconscious mind is always working, even when you're sleeping!

It controls things like breathing, your heartbeat, and even your habits!

The more seeds you plant, the bigger and stronger they grow!

If you imagine something scary, your subconscious reacts as if it's really happening!

That's why movies can make you cry or jump, even though they're not real!

Here's how to use your garden wisely!

Plant good seeds!
Think positive thoughts, like "I am kind!" or "I can learn anything!"

So, your subconscious mind is like a garden where your thoughts grow! Make sure you're planting flowers, not weeds!

Here are some good seeds you can plant every day!

I can do hard things and keep trying.

Every day is a new chance to do my best.

I respect myself and others.

My heart is full of good things.

I look for the good in myself and in others.

Glossary:

Subconscious Mind: The part of your mind that works quietly in the background, like a hidden garden where seeds (ideas) grow, even when you're not thinking about them.

Conscious Mind: The part of your mind that you use to think and make choices, like when you decide what to eat or how to play. It's like the gardener who picks which seeds to plant.

Affirmations: Short, happy sentences you say to yourself, like "I am strong" or "I can do this!" They're like water and sunshine that help good thoughts grow.

Confidence: Believing in yourself and knowing you can do something, like trying something new or learning to ride a bike. It's like planting seeds of bravery in your mind.

Gl*ssary:

Habits: Things you do over and over, like brushing your teeth every morning or saying "thank you." They're like planting the same kind of seed every day until it grows into a big, strong plant.

Thoughts: Ideas or pictures in your mind, like imagining your favorite ice cream or remembering a fun day. They're the tiny seeds that can grow into big feelings or actions.

Beliefs: The things you think are true, like "I am kind" or "I can make friends." They're like the roots of a plant, holding it in place and helping it grow strong.

Affirmations are short, happy sentences
that you can say to yourself!
Can you write down 5 affirmations?

1 _____

2 _____

3 _____

4 _____

5 _____

Can you help the bee get to the flower?

Lacey L. Bakker is a best-selling author who believes the mind is like a magical garden where positive thoughts grow! As the founder of Pandamonium Publishing House, Lacey and her team create inspiring books and love helping kids plant seeds of confidence, kindness, and imagination. When she's not writing, she enjoys spending time with her family, hiking with her dog, and travelling.

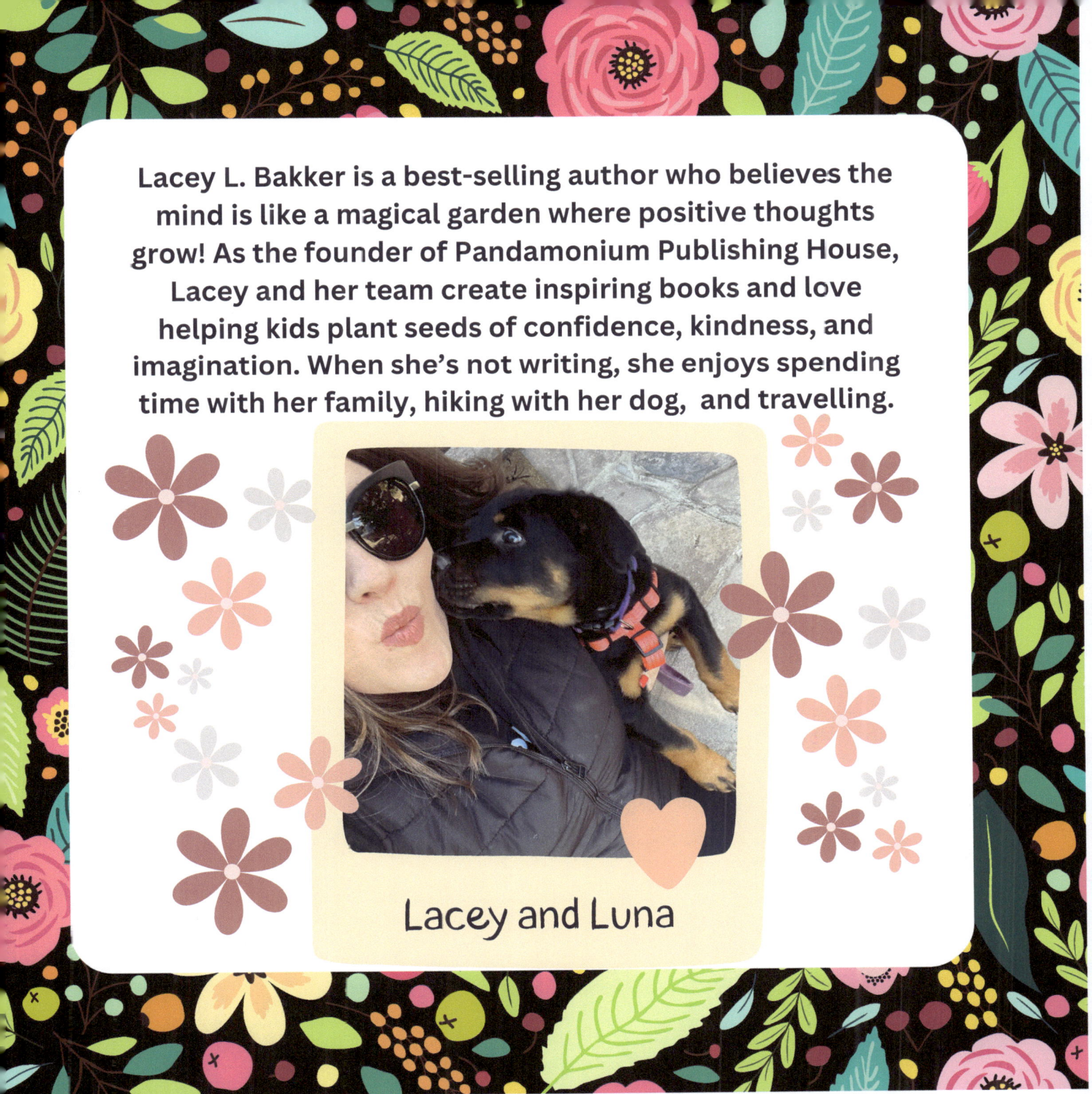

Lacey and Luna